EUROPE

Siberia

● Novosibirsk

ASIA

AFRICA

AUSTRALIA

Pushinka
the Barking Fox

A True Story of Unexpected Friendship

by Lee Alan Dugatkin and Lyudmila Trut

PERSNICKETY PRESS

Designed by Shan Stumpf
Edited by Caroline Watkins

Library of Congress
Cataloging-in-Publication
Data available.

ISBN: 978-1-943978-46-5

Printed in Canada at Friesens Corporation
cpsia tracking label information
Production Location: Altona, Manitoba
Production Date: 8/2/2019
Cohort: Batch No. 255073

10 9 8 7 6 5 4 3 2 1

Produced by Persnickety Press
An imprint of WunderMill, Inc.
120A North Salem Street
Apex, NC 27502

Dedicated to Lyudmila's
friends—the loving, adorable
tame foxes of Siberia.

Lee Alan Dugatkin

www.wundermillbooks.com

Pushinka
the Barking Fox

A True Story of Unexpected Friendship

by Lee Alan Dugatkin and Lyudmila Trut

PERSNICKETY PRESS

The Experiment

Pushinka's story really began years before her birth, with the start of a domestication experiment in 1959 under Dr. Dmitri Belyaev. In the years following, a team of scientists, led by Dr. Lyudmila Trut, tested thousands of foxes, measuring how friendly each fox was towards people. For example, if a fox wagged its tail or came over to be petted when a person approached, that fox got a high score; if it growled or ran away, it got a low score.

After Lyudmila and her team chose the very friendliest of the foxes—the ones with the highest scores—those foxes were selected to produce pups for the next year in the experiment. When those pups grew up and reached one year old, they were tested for friendliness to people, same as their parents, and the friendliest of those foxes were again selected to produce their own pups. Lyudmila's team has done this every year for sixty years, and the experiment continues today!

"You become responsible,
forever, for what you have tamed."

— The Little Prince by Antoine de Saint-Exupéry

LYUDMILA

DR. DMITRI BELYAEV

FOX PUP

DMITRI AND PUSHINKA

In a small house in Siberia, just big enough for two, lived a scientist and a fox. For thousands of years, people have turned wild animals into pets, and this scientist wanted to understand that process. So, in one of the coldest places on earth, she joined an experiment to make a new kind of pet—a tame fox—and 15 years later, she moved in with one.

This is the true story of a life-changing friendship. This is Lyudmila and Pushinka's story.

Lyudmila, the scientist, studied lots of cute fox pups on the fox farm, but Pushinka stood out. She was the sweetest pup Lyudmila had ever met, and beautiful, too, with shiny silver-black fur, a white stripe on her face, and black eyes. Pushinka would wag her tail and run to lick Lyudmila when she approached the fox farm. Lyudmila fell in love with her immediately.

Lyudmila and Penka

Lyudmila and foxes

By the time Pushinka turned one year old, she was ready to have her own pups. Lyudmila moved her from the fox farm into a two-bedroom house—with one room just for Pushinka—and their friendship continued to grow. With every treat, long walk, and game of fetch, Pushinka, whose ancestors had been wild foxes, trusted Lyudmila more and more.

When Pushinka gave birth to her six pups, she brought them to meet Lyudmila—something wild foxes would never do. Lyudmila could not believe it.

But love, you see, surprises us.

Lyudmila made space in her home and her heart for her six pups—Penka, Prelest, Pesna, Plaksa, Palma, and Pushok—and watched in awe as the tiny pups developed personalities and preferences.

Pushinka, who had become a gentle, caring mother, was always watching. Lyudmila was proud of her friend.

Lyudmila kept a journal nearby, filling it with careful notes on the ways her beloved foxes were growing and changing.

Left page (partially cut off)

...e sofa reading a magazine.
...toy, played with it for a long
...feet and peacefully fell asleep.

...se Pushinka greeted me,
...inviting me to play, running

...around and then hiding the
...it from the closet and runs
...de it so no one can find it.
...very cheerful, running

...moves the pups as close
...rson in the experiment)
...e the fact that she
...im with her most

...ling her tail and
...any. She is always
...she lays at my feet

...und the house. I
...with my hand,
...my shoulder.

...running to me

...me around
...ing.

Right page

June 24, 1974: Prelest approached me very trustingly, laid down on the bench and stayed there for a long time, right next to me.

June 30, 1974: More and more Penka and Pushok are trying to communicate with me. All morning Penka played beside me, inviting me to play with her ball. Pushinka settled under a canopy near me again. Penka came running, jumped on the coach, licked my ears, and then went to Pushinka.

July 7, 1974: Penka is looking for more interactions with me. She is always walking with me and "saying" something (gu-gu-gaak). When she sits by me, she strives to get my attention. She crawls under my arm so I'll pet her. She tickles my nose, cheeks, lips, and ears. I laugh at all the things she is doing.

July 15, 1974: Pushinka is playing with the pups. Adorable.

July 30, 1974: If one of the pups jumps on my lap, the second one is pulling the first one away, the third one is pulling away the second one, and so on.

September 9, 1974: Penka and Pushok are romping around with me. They play with each other, but only when they are by my side. Penka pesters Pushok; she won't leave him alone. Pushok wants to hide behind me (on the sofa) or under my robe, so Penka won't let him there.

September 13, 1974: Pushinka and the pups met me with joy. What did they do?! They climbed on my knees and jumped over my head. They are so busy!

November 1, 1974: Pushinka smelled my robe for a long time, then just like a dog, stretched herself out and lay on my lap.

November 6, 1974: Pushinka tried to squeeze herself under my ro... lay on my lap, and stayed like that for a while as ?... behind her ears.

Palma loved to jump on tables; Plaksa didn't like to be petted; and Prelest was a bit of a troublemaker. Pushok wouldn't let Lyudmila out of his sight, but it was little Penka whom she loved the most. Some nights, Lyudmila would rock Penka in her arms until she drifted off to sleep. They were happy in their small house in Siberia, big enough for eight.

Plaksa

Prelest

Pesna

Penka

Palma

Pushok

Meanwhile, on the fox farm, Lyudmila's team was learning a lot about domestication through their experiment and daily interaction with the foxes. The scientists observed that the foxes were calmer and friendlier to people than their wild ancestors had been. Just like dogs, they licked people's hands and rolled on their backs for tummy rubs. The scientists also noticed that some of the foxes had floppy ears, and some had curly tails—they had started to look more like dogs, too!

At home with Pushinka, Lyudmila continued to learn about her fuzzy friend. Pushinka had grown very attached to Lyudmila and did not like to share her with other foxes. When Lyudmila brought another tame fox, Rada, to visit the house, Pushinka became jealous and angry. She pushed Rada out of the house and refused to let Lyudmila pet her. Lyudmila was worried. Had she broken Pushinka's trust?

But love, you see, bonds us...

As time passed and the snow thawed, so too did Pushinka's displeasure with Lyudmila. On warm summer evenings, the two friends would sit side by side beneath the stars. They spent many nights like that—Lyudmila reading, Pushinka dozing—enjoying the gentler Siberian season together. One such night, unexpected footsteps approached the house. Pushinka tensed and charged in the direction of the unfamiliar sound.

Silence.

And then...

Pushinka began to BARK, warning the stranger not to come closer. She was protecting Lyudmila, as devoted to her master as any dog would be. The scientist was stunned. Wild foxes DON'T bark!

But love, you see, changes us.

At 85-years-old, Lyudmila still leads the experiment in Siberia, but she has never loved another fox the way that she loved Pushinka and her pups. Between 1974 and 1977, the brood of foxes living with Lyudmila expanded to include Pushinka's many grandchildren—more fox pups

to study and love. Later, after the deaths of her fuzzy friends, it became harder and harder for Lyudmila to return to the little house in Siberia, just big enough for two...then eight... then none. Still, Lyudmila remembers her years spent with Pushinka and the pups as among the best of her life.

Pushinka, descendant of wild foxes, became *woman's best friend.*

Love had changed her, too.

FROM WILD TO TAME.

We Have Tamed Animals for Many Reasons

For centuries, people have tamed many different wild animals. Every time our ancestors tamed a species, they had a goal in mind—horses provided transportation; oxen helped us with farm work; cows were sources of milk and meat; and cats killed pests that could be harmful to people and crops.

Tamed species share many things in common. Like the tame foxes, many tamed species have floppy ears, curly tails, and many different color patterns in their fur or on their skin. Scientists think choosing the calmest animals leads to the physical changes we see in tamed species, and though they are not exactly sure how or why, they are doing experiments to understand this better.

Chemical Changes in the Tame Foxes

Lyudmila and her team noticed changes in the foxes' appearance, but changes also occurred inside the foxes. One important change they observed was in the levels of certain chemicals in the foxes' bodies. Hormones are chemicals that control many things in animals, including their emotions. High levels of one hormone, called cortisol, lead to nervous and stressed behavior in foxes. Lyudmila discovered that tame foxes only have half as much cortisol as wild foxes.

Not only are tame foxes less nervous and stressed, but they may be happier too. Another hormone, called serotonin, is linked with good feelings in animals. The tame foxes have much higher levels of serotonin than foxes in the wild.

THE EXPERIMENT CONTINUES...

What's Next for the Tame Foxes?

This is one of the longest running experiments in history. Every year, Lyudmila and her team in Siberia still test hundreds of foxes and choose the friendliest foxes to produce pups for the next experiment. The scientists keep track of changes in what the foxes look like and how they behave. They are also studying DNA—the chemical building blocks that make up all life on earth—to understand how taming has led to changes in the DNA of their foxes.

Lyudmila and her team work with scientists from all over the world. They are always thinking of new questions about the tame foxes and coming up with new ways to answer them. The fox experiment is now in its sixtieth year, and with a little bit of luck, it will continue for another sixty years—and beyond!

Photo Credits

All photos are from The Institute of Cytology and Genetics, Novosibirsk, Russia, with the exception of:

Pages 4-5, Fox farm: Aaron Dugatkin; Inset photo: The Institute of Cytology and Genetics, Novosibirsk, Russia

Page 8, Two foxes playing in snow: Aaron Dugatkin; All other photos on page 8: The Institute of Cytology and Genetics, Novosibirsk, Russia

Page 29, Lyudmila holding a journal: Aaron Dugatkin